D0912945

DISCARDED OR WITHDRAWN
GREAT NECK LIBRARY

J/551.48/N

MAR 26 2013

GREAT NECK LIBRARY
GREAT NECK, NY 11023
(516) 466-8055
www.greatnecklibrary.org

OUR CHANGING EARTH

RIVERS, LAKES, AND OCEANS

Jason D. Nemeth

PowerKiDS press™

New York

GREAT NECK LIBRARY

Published in 2012 by The Rosen Publishing Group, Inc.
29 East 21st Street, New York, NY 10010

Copyright © 2012 by The Rosen Publishing Group, Inc.

All rights reserved. No part of this book may be reproduced in any form without permission in writing from the publisher, except by a reviewer.

First Edition

Editor: Amelie von Zumbusch
Book Design: Greg Tucker

Photo Credits: Cover, pp. 4–5, 6, 7, 8–9, 10–11, 11 (top, bottom), 13, 14, 15, 16–17, 18, 19 (left, right), 20, 22 Shutterstock.com; p. 9 (main) by Greg Tucker; p. 12 Dorling Kindersley/Getty Images; p. 21 DigitalGlobe via Getty Images.

Library of Congress Cataloging-in-Publication Data

Nemeth, Jason D.
 Rivers, lakes, and oceans / by Jason D. Nemeth. — 1st ed.
    p. cm. — (Our changing earth)
 Includes index.
 ISBN 978-1-4488-6171-2 (library binding) — ISBN 978-1-4488-6300-6 (pbk.) —
 ISBN 978-1-4488-6301-3 (6-pack)
 1. Rivers—Juvenile literature. 2. Lakes—Juvenile literature. 3. Ocean—Juvenile literature. I. Title.
 GB1203.8.N46 2012
 551.48—dc23
                              2011026316

Manufactured in the United States of America

CPSIA Compliance Information: Batch #WW12PK: For Further Information contact Rosen Publishing, New York, New York at 1-800-237-9932

CONTENTS

About 70 percent of Earth's surface is covered by water. There is water in lakes, ponds, rivers, and oceans. There is water in the air and in the ground. There is even water in our bodies! There is so much water that if you could roll it all into a big ball, it would be 860 miles (1,384 km) wide.

Scientists are not certain how Earth ended up with so much water. Some think that big, icy rocks from outer space brought water when they crashed on Earth. Scientists are certain about one thing, though. Life on Earth would not exist without water.

There are more than 250,000 rivers in the United States. The Colorado River, seen here, is about 1,450 miles (2,334 km) long. It is the country's seventh-longest river.

WATER WORLD

Water is special in many ways. It is the only substance on Earth's surface that appears naturally as a liquid, solid, and gas. Liquid water is what we drink and swim in. Ice and snow are solid water. **Water vapor** is water that is a gas. It can be found in the air as steam. It makes the stickiness you feel on a hot day, too.

This iceberg is made of water that is a solid, while the ocean around it is liquid water. Icebergs are big pieces of floating ice. They are mostly underwater.

When you boil water to cook, some of it turns into steam. You can often see steam rising from a pot of boiling water.

Water is very **stable**. This means it does not change easily. The ocean will not boil away on a hot day. A cold day will not freeze it through. This means water is always there for plants and animals in whatever form they need it.

WATER RECYCLED

The same water has been on Earth for millions of years. It is always changing its form and moving around. This is called the **water cycle**.

When it gets heated by the Sun, liquid water in the oceans and elsewhere **evaporates**. This means that the water turns to gas and rises into the air.

Snow is made of tiny pieces of ice, called snowflakes. Snowflakes form when water vapor in the air turns to ice. When rain turns to ice as it falls, sleet forms.

Later, the water vapor cools down and forms clouds. It falls on land as rain and snow. The rain and melted snow fill up lakes, streams, and rivers. In time, the rivers return the water to the oceans. Then the cycle starts again.

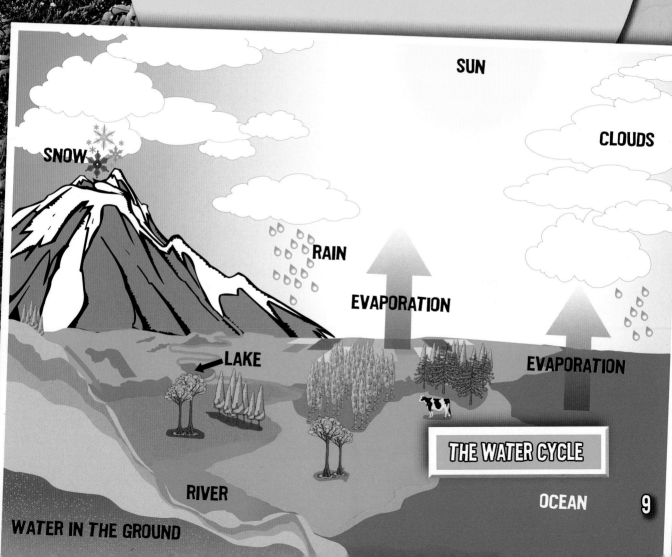

SUN

CLOUDS

SNOW

RAIN

EVAPORATION

EVAPORATION

LAKE

THE WATER CYCLE

RIVER

OCEAN

WATER IN THE GROUND

WATER, WATER EVERYWHERE

The oceans hold almost 97 percent of the water on Earth. Ocean water is salt water. This is water in which salt has become part of the liquid. This happens because oceans are fed by rivers. The rivers wash salt and other **minerals** from the rocks on land into the ocean.

The **sea level**, or height of the oceans, changes over time. It also goes up and down each day with the tides. Tides are caused by the Moon's **gravity** pulling on Earth's waters. Gravity is a force the pulls objects together. Earth's gravity keeps us from floating off into space.

Sea turtles drink seawater. Their bodies take the salt out of the water. The turtles have salt glands near their eyes. These body parts get rid of the salt from the water the turtles drink.

The tides are stronger in some places than others. Mont-Saint-Michel, in France, has very strong tides. Here you can see Mont-Saint-Michel at low tide (top) and at high tide (left).

OCEANS AND CLIMATE

Oceans cover more than half of Earth's surface. This means that most of the sunlight that falls on Earth falls on its oceans. The oceans soak up the Sun's heat. Ocean currents help spread this heat around. This makes certain places warmer than they would otherwise be.

The ocean also soaks up gases from the **atmosphere**, such as **carbon dioxide**. The atmosphere is the layers of air around Earth.

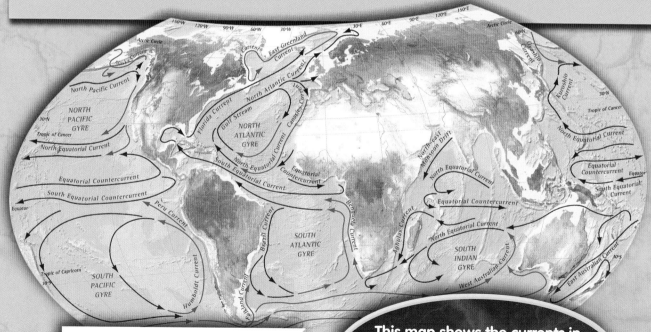

MAP OF OCEAN CURRENTS

This map shows the currents in Earth's oceans. The red arrows are warm currents, while the blue ones are cold currents.

Carbon dioxide traps the Sun's heat inside the atmosphere. This makes the planet warmer. Without the ocean, there would be much more carbon dioxide in the air. Earth would be much warmer.

A warm ocean current called the North Atlantic Current makes Ireland much warmer than it would otherwise be.

IT'S ALL DOWNHILL

Wherever it can, water flows downward. This happens because of the pull of Earth's gravity. Oceans cover the lowest parts of Earth's **crust**, or outside. Rivers and streams flow downhill. Lakes and ponds form when water pools in low areas, such as valleys.

Many caves have water in them. This underground lake is in a cave in Hamilton Parish, Bermuda.

Gravity also pulls water underground. However, a layer of rock traps it before it gets too deep. Underground water, called **groundwater**, fills spaces between pieces of rock and soil. There is about 100 times more freshwater underground than there is in all Earth's lakes and rivers combined. Freshwater is water that is not salty. It is the kind of water people drink.

Water always flows downhill. This sets the paths in which rivers and streams flow.

Some of the water from rainfall or melted snow sinks into the soil to become groundwater. Some runs off into streams and rivers. The land from which a body of water receives water is its **watershed**.

Much of the water that runs off Earth's surface flows into small streams, such as creeks and brooks. These small streams usually flow into bigger streams and rivers, which may flow into even larger rivers. Large rivers often empty into oceans.

Water changes land as it flows across it. It carves valleys through rock. It also carries rocks and soil from one place to another.

The Hudson River flows into Upper New York Bay, as seen here. Water from the bay flows through the Narrows into Lower New York Bay and then into the Atlantic Ocean.

LAKES, PONDS, AND WETLANDS

Lakes and ponds form in places where water builds up. This happens when water flows into a low spot more quickly than it can flow out of it. It also happens in places that are surrounded by high land.

Most lakes are freshwater. Lakes with no streams flowing out of them may be saltwater. Streams wash

The Great Salt Lake, in Utah, is North America's largest saltwater lake. It is even saltier than Earth's oceans are!

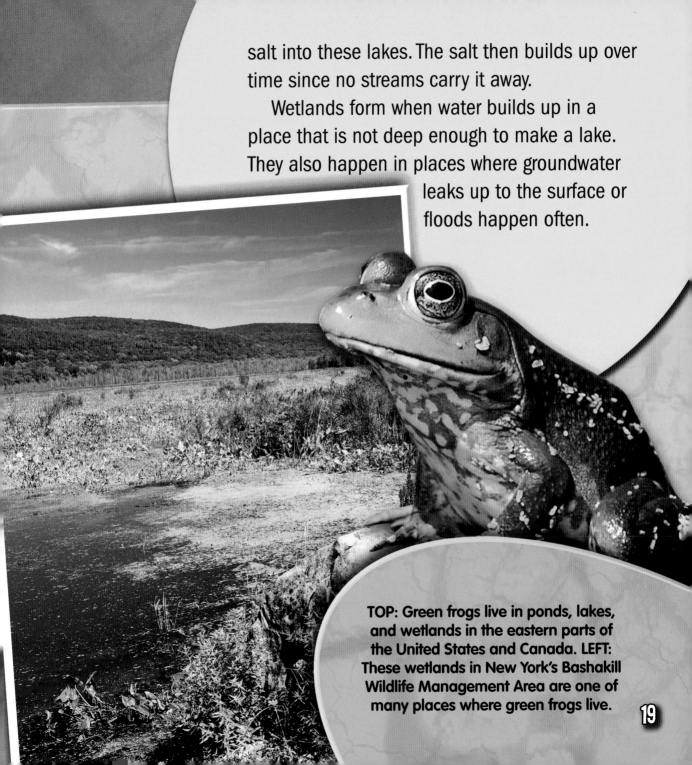

salt into these lakes. The salt then builds up over time since no streams carry it away.

Wetlands form when water builds up in a place that is not deep enough to make a lake. They also happen in places where groundwater leaks up to the surface or floods happen often.

TOP: Green frogs live in ponds, lakes, and wetlands in the eastern parts of the United States and Canada. LEFT: These wetlands in New York's Bashakill Wildlife Management Area are one of many places where green frogs live.

DIRTY WATER

Clean water is necessary for life. People are doing things that pollute Earth's water, though. Pollution comes from many places. Litter, such as plastic bags and bottles, may end up in lakes and streams. Many of these flow to the oceans. Farms use chemicals like **pesticides** to kill bugs. Pesticides stay in the soil and sink down into the groundwater. Factories send smoke into the

As you can see, this river is polluted with a lot of trash. Some towns hold clean-up days on which people pick up trash from rivers and riverbanks.

air. This falls back down with the rain and pollutes the land and the water.

Pollution can make water unsafe for people to drink. It can also kill plants and animals that live in or near the water.

Oil spills also pollute Earth's waters. This picture of an oil spill in the Gulf of Mexico in 2010 was taken from high above.

WILL THERE BE ENOUGH?

Pollution is not the only water problem. As more people live on Earth, they need more and more water to cook, drink, and clean. Some places do not have very much water to start with. Other places have lots of water but waste it.

Freshwater is only a tiny part of all of Earth's water. We need to use it wisely so that there is enough for all of the people and other living things that need it.

Kids should drink several cups of water every day. Water keeps you healthy!

GLOSSARY

atmosphere (AT-muh-sfeer) The gases around an object in space. On Earth this is air.

carbon dioxide (KAHR-bun dy-OK-syd) A gas that has no smell or taste. People breathe out carbon dioxide.

crust (KRUST) The outside of a planet.

evaporates (ih-VA-puh-rayts) Changes from a liquid, like water, to a gas, like steam.

gravity (GRA-vih-tee) The natural force that causes objects to move toward the center of Earth.

groundwater (GROWND-wah-tur) Water that is found underground, where all of the air spaces in the soil and rock are filled with water.

minerals (MIN-rulz) Kinds of natural matter that are not animals, plants, or other living things.

pesticides (PES-tuh-sydz) Poisons used to kill pests.

sea level (SEE LEH-vul) The height of the ocean.

stable (STAY-bul) Not easily moved or changed.

water cycle (WAH-ter SY-kul) The natural process of water drying up and forming clouds then falling back to Earth as rain.

watershed (WAW-ter-shed) The land from which water runs off into a certain body of water.

water vapor (WAH-ter VAY-pur) The gaseous state of water.

INDEX

WEB SITES

Due to the changing nature of Internet links, PowerKids Press has developed an online list of Web sites related to the subject of this book. This site is updated regularly. Please use this link to access the list:
www.powerkidslinks.com/chng/rivers/